CROSBY &
BLUNDELLSANDS

THROUGH TIME

Hugh Hollinghurst

AMBERLEY PUBLISHING

Acknowledgements

To Peter Owen, who generously allowed me to use his collection of postcards, took many of the present day photographs and helped to organise the images.

To the late Mike Stammers and John Cochrane for information provided by their recent publications *Crosby Curiosities* and *Mills, Mollies & Marl Pits*.

To the Local History Unit of the Crosby Library, the *Crosby Herald*, Roger Hull, and the Crosby and District Historical Society for their help and use of archive photographs, and to all who have conributed archive images and in particular Sefton Libraries for those on pages 5, 8, 64, 86, 90 and 94.

To my wife Joan, Crosby born and bred, who has proofread and been a great source of encouragement, information and reminiscences.

First published 2013

Amberley Publishing
The Hill, Stroud, Gloucestershire, GL5 4EP
www.amberley-books.com

Copyright © Hugh Hollinghurst, 2013

The right of Hugh Hollinghurst to be identified as the
Author of this work has been asserted in accordance with
the Copyrights, Designs and Patents Act 1988.

ISBN 978 1 4456 1340 6 (print)
ISBN 978 1 4456 1352 9 (ebook)

British Library Cataloguing in Publication Data.
A catalogue record for this book is available from the
British Library.

Typesetting by Amberley Publishing.
Printed in Great Britain.

Introduction

Until the mid-eighteenth century, Crosby was a remote, rural community, remarkable only for the chapel of St Michael (dependent on Sefton church), the school (founded in 1620), the mill and Crosby Hall, home of the Blundell family. In 1835, the curate wrote to his brother: 'Do come, if it be for no other purpose to see how, & at what sort of place, I am doomed to spend my days upon earth.' Travelling the five miles to Liverpool necessitated going via muddy track, shore or the Leeds & Liverpool Canal.

Great and Little Crosby were separate townships, and stayed so until becoming one urban district in 1932. Each had its own distinct identity, the original boundary stone on the corner of Little Crosby Road and Oakfield Avenue recalling old rivalries and modern differences. Little Crosby was, and still is, a delightful time warp, a tiny Catholic community inextricably linked to Crosby Hall. At the heart of Great Crosby was the green with the cross of St Michael, by which the Vikings had distinguished the community ('the village by the cross').

When the railway arrived in 1848, Nicholas Blundell steered the line away from the two villages, and his home, by offering the company free land for construction of the railway on unproductive, sandy soil nearer the sea. Then, between the railway and the sea, accessible to the station, the Blundells developed a superior housing estate that grew into Blundellsands. The railway wrought huge changes. Professional classes came to live in the area and the service industry increased. Great Crosby expanded to take its present shape: north along Pinfold Lane (now Cooks Road); south along Liverpool Road towards Liverpool; east along Moor Lane past the mill to Thornton and Sefton; and west down Thorps Lane (now Coronation Road) and Out Lane (now Victoria Road) towards the station and the shore. In 1853, St Luke's church was built to replace St Michael's chapel and accommodate the growing population, forming a parish of its own, followed eventually by other grand Anglican, Catholic, Methodist, Congregational and Presbyterian churches. In 1878, Merchant Taylors' School was raised from its nadir of four pupils to a grand building on a fresh spacious site for two hundred; the old school building was used by the girls as the basis for their school, founded in 1888. They were joined along Liverpool Road by St Mary's College, Seafield Convent (Grammar) School (now Sacred Heart Catholic College), and Stanfield, Merchant Taylors' School for Girls' junior department.

The Victorian and Edwardian residential developments along the primary arterial roads outlined above were followed by a vast expansion of well-planned housing between them, largely semidetached and tree-lined. Post war, few large-scale sites have been developed and the building of homes has consisted of filling in the gaps. All the roads have been well maintained and the houses well kept. Residential Crosby has maintained its character, standards and leafy looks.

Meanwhile, the Blundellsands estate was most successful in drawing wealthy businessmen to build their homes on a grand scale along the coast. They attracted, and were attracted by, a grand overall 'serpentine' design, golf course, rugby club, tennis club, Anglican, Catholic and Presbyterian churches, and other social amenities, uncontaminated by shops or pubs, except for the Blundellsands Hotel. Sir William Forwood's home boasted two remarkable fountains in his garden and one visitor (the First Lord of the Admiralty) enthused that the view equalled that of the bay of Naples. Since then, his home and many others were demolished and apartment blocks rose in their place. Those closest to the sea were destroyed by the waywardness of the River Alt, and on their debris a seafront established. But just enough remains for Blundellsands to retain its distinctive character.

This cannot be said for the centre of the 'village' – as it is still called – of (Great) Crosby, which has been almost unrecognisably altered from a century ago, described in a guide book as 'picturesque'. The green has long gone and the original site of the cross, which has been moved, obliterated. The last of the sixteenth-century thatched cottages were destroyed as recently as 1963. This century, 20 per cent of the premises have been demolished, with no hope of resurrection, or are now lying vacant, and the sites that are let change with ever increasing and bewildering rapidity. Between 1970 and 1998, nearly 70 per cent of shops in the centre of Great Crosby changed not just ownership but the nature of their business. By 2012 (only half the length of period previously surveyed), the figure was nearly 50 per cent. Central Buildings were the victim of the property speculation that led up to the financial crisis of 2008, bought up in the hope of lucrative development that never transpired. These and many other sites are a derelict eyesore, despite cosmetic attempts to disguise the damage – a tribute to the abortive plan by Sainsbury's to develop a superstore.

However, the peaceful and attractive nature of Great Crosby's residential areas and all of Little Crosby remains. It is hoped that this book will help remind the community of the past, appreciate today what has survived and encourage them to preserve the best for future generations.

Crosby & Blundellsands Through Time takes you on a journey from the village of Great Crosby with a circular perambulation, through the township, and up Moor Lane to Thornton, Sefton and Ince Blundell. Starting again at Blundellsands and Crosby station, we travel through Blundellsands along the seafront to Little Crosby and finish at Hightown.

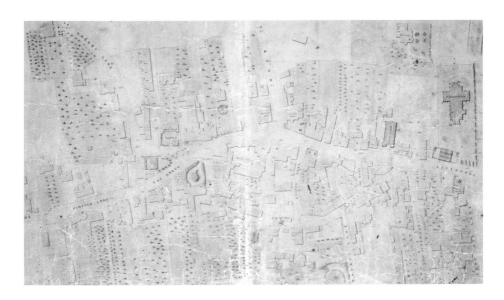

Crosby Village

In this map of 1864 (orientated east), St Luke's Halsall School appears on the left above Pinfold Lane (now Cooks Road). At the other end of the lane is the 'Constabulary' on the edge of the Green. On the opposite corner is St Michael's Well and Cross. Further south is Church Road, which takes its name from St Michael's chapel, of which only the tower remains at the north-west end. Going from there along Islington to Liverpool Road, you come to St Luke's church on the right of the map with the Vicarage to the east of it. The aerial photograph, taken around 2000, covers the same area. The police station is now occupied by Sainsbury's, and the Green by NatWest Bank, Iceland and a car park. Islington has been extended and widened to create a north–south bypass to the west. Central Buildings lines the south of Church Road. Moor Lane has been pedestrianised, together with Liverpool Road as far as the east–west bypass, marked by the line of The Weint ('alleyway') on the 1864 map.

The Village with the Cross

St Michael's Cross now stands next to the NatWest bank with an explanatory plaque (left of the NatWest logo). From time immemorial, there was a well here, whose healing waters were dedicated with a cross to St Michael. Viking invaders christened it Crosby ('the village with the cross'). The cross originally stood on the village green, as shown in the picture above, but in 1986 it was restored and moved north by 50 yards. Rededicated in 2000, the stone base is far older than the wooden cross, which dates from June 2012 when its predecessor was vandalised.

St Michael's Cross

On the village green, St Michael's Cross is pictured with Clifton Avenue appearing at the gap between the terraced houses/shops in the centre of the photograph. The 'avenue' survives as a shortcut from the car park to Liverpool Road. Note the preservation of the basic structure of the buildings either side of the alleyway and the original brick patterning round the windows on the left. However, on the right the added top storey has destroyed the delightful dormer windows.

Police Station

We look down Cooks Road towards the scene in the next archive photograph, courtesy of Sefton Libraries. The tramlines have disappeared, but the tram posts are still there, used for lighting. Notice the advertisement hoarding also featured, from the other side, in the photograph of Cooks Road cottage. The old police station was demolished to make way for road improvements and Sainsbury's in the 1970s. Nearby was the pound or pinfold, where stray animals were kept by the pinder until ransomed. Hence Pinfold Lane, now Cooks Road, and Pinfold Court on the corner of Alexandra Road and Cooks Road.

Cooks Road Tram Terminus

The tram service run by the Liverpool Overhead Railway between 1900 and 1925 connected Crosby with its Seaforth Sands station. On the right is the Grapes Hotel (demolished in 1912) advertising Thorougood's beer, brewed at their works in Queen Street, Waterloo. On the other corner is Alcock's, first in a series of grocers alongside Irwin's, Edward's and Spar. Since then it has been pet shop, a bike shop and a boutique. Just to the right, off picture, is St Luke's Halsall Primary School.

St Luke's Halsall Church of England Primary School

An infants' class of 1870 contrasts with after school play in 2012 (inset: a relic of 1883 building). In her will of 1758, Catherine Halsall endowed a school for girls to be taught reading, knitting and sewing. Known first as the Girls' School, then as the Mistress's School and Halsall School, it was finally attached to St Luke's parish as St Luke's Halsall School. When the boys from St Luke's Boys' School joined in 1972, it was the oldest girls school in Lancashire.

Cooks Road Cottage

Ornamental tram posts overlook a passing loop and pedestrians of all ages along the cobbled road. Opposite are arcaded shops and one of Crosby's thatched cottages, possibly from Elizabethan times, the last of which was demolished in 1963. An advertisement hoarding stands on the corner of Alexandra Road with St Luke's spire in the distance. The police station is just round the corner to the left; the Birkey Hotel and St Luke's Halsall School are behind you to the right and left respectively.

Liverpool Road from Clifton Avenue to the Bank Buildings

Miss Brennan, pawnbroker, stands by Moor Place, as it was known then, now Clifton Avenue (between Nos. 9 and 11 Liverpool Road, not Cooks Road as on the photograph). The door to the entrance of her premises can still be seen in the grandiosely named passageway, surely the narrowest avenue in the world. Further along, on the corner, is the old George Hotel and opposite is the mock-Tudor façade of Bank Buildings, originally Martins, then subsumed in to Barclays, and finally converted to a bar.

St Michael's Chapel

The last of the chapels associated with St Michael's Cross, built in 1770, is depicted by Herdman above (courtesy of Graham Hignett and Liverpool Libraries). Standing in the foreground of the scene below, it was demolished after St Luke's church was consecrated in 1853. Church Road, to which it gave its name, is pictured to the right of both images. This has now disappeared as a named road, as there are no premises facing it following the recent demolition of Central Buildings.

St Luke's Church of England Boy's Primary School

Notice the embryonic extension to the car park and construction of a new carriageway, now converted into the bus station. This photograph of St Luke's Boy's School was taken shortly before its demolition in 1974, when it was merged with St Luke's Halsall. Bricks from St Michael's chapel were used in the construction of the Boy's School in 1871, and then, appropriately, recycled again to form a commemorative seat with explanatory inscription outside St Luke's church, the successor of the chapel.

St Helen's Church

A view taken inside St Luke's Boy's School playground at the last school bazaar held in 1973, the year before it closed and was then demolished to make way for a car park. Beyond the wall is the old St Helen's church built in 1930, already showing signs of impending demolition. The new St Helen's is visible under the awning being constructed and the result can be seen in the photograph below. It has already lasted nearly as long as its predecessor.

The George Hotel

Built in 1929, when the old building was demolished for road widening, the George poses as a half-timbered manor house in Tudor or Elizabethan times, complementing Bank Buildings opposite. Caught before pedestrianisation in 1995, motorists, shoppers and cyclists coexist amicably, while Costigan's advertises bacon in competition with butchers McNamee over the road. Church Road on the left is fully navigable but in reverse direction to today, as the no entry sign shows. Now only the George plies its traditional trade.

Moor Lane

We look down Moor Lane towards the junction with Liverpool Road. A tram passes on its way from Cooks Road to Seaforth Sands station (not vice versa, as can be seen by the direction of the electricity collector) so the photograph was taken before 1926. On the right at the junction is the old George Hotel, but all other establishments have changed in nature. The new build on the left contrasts with splendid old dormer windows still towering over the block on the right.

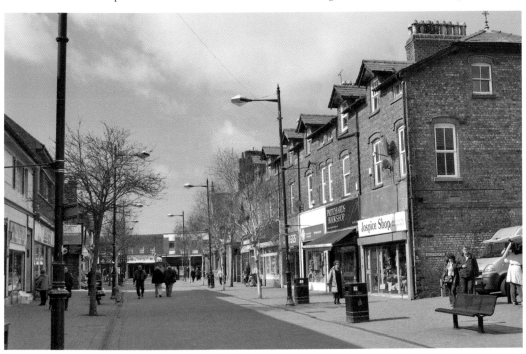

THE VILLAGE, CROSBY.   H.9944.

Crown and Central Buildings

The bus stop on the right shows that the old photograph, with as many cyclists as vehicles, was taken before the bypass opened in 1958. On the left, with its arcade still in position, Crown Buildings sports its unique and strange mix of Flemish gable, mock-Tudor timbering, pebble dash and comical, conical corner turrets. Between it and Costigan's can be glimpsed the end of Central Buildings, now demolished. Princess Diana's garden is now in the foreground on the right.

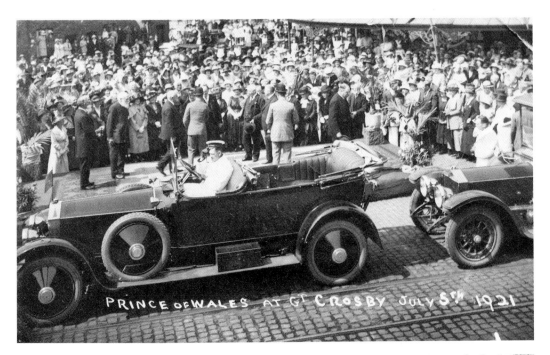

PRINCE OF WALES AT G^t CROSBY JULY 5th 1921

Royalty Remembered
The Prince of Wales visits
Crosby on a tour of the
area after opening docks at
Liverpool. Lord Derby is in
attendance and VIPs queue up
to be presented to the Prince on
a dais erected by the Boulder
Stone. The shop arcading of
Crown Buildings, top right, and
the tram lines at the bottom,
show the parameters of the
photograph. A commemorative
flower bed, planted in memory
of Princess Diana, now provides
a colourful welcome to the
pedestrian shopping precinct.

LIVERPOOL ROAD
GT CROSBY
1832

The Boulder Stone

The 18-ton Boulder Stone of white
gypsum, brought down from the
Lake District by a glacier, was
unearthed 20 feet down in a quarry
by Cook's Lane (now Manor Road).
In 1898, Mellard Reade persuaded
the District Council to transport it
to this site. After fifteen horses had
failed to draw it, a traction engine
was anchored to the trolley, whose
wheels churned up the lane 'like a
mortar mill' to orientate it as it had
lain in the boulder clay. Note (above)
the Blackledge's (baker's) advert and
the tram, tracks and post to carry
the electric wires. Only one trace
remains of any of these: a stump of
one of the original posts stands to
this day (left) opposite St Peter and
Paul's church further along Liverpool
Road, possibly kept originally as a
stench pipe for a sewer, but now
blocked up.

Crown Buildings

By 1924 the boulder was considered a severe obstruction to traffic, and the council proposed to break it up. The Liverpool Geological Society protested, with the recommendation that it be moved to a public park. The view above shows the full extent of Crown Buildings after the stone had been removed to Coronation Park and had been replaced by a mini-roundabout. On the left is one end of Central Buildings. The trams have also disappeared, along with their tracks and posts, and been replaced by a bus service operated by Ribble.

The Old Parsonage

The white-faced cottage was built as a parsonage for the incumbent of St Michael's chapel in 1668, on glebe land upon which St Luke's church was later constructed with its expanded graveyard. The curate of St Michael's would till the land in addition to his church duties and also act as Headmaster of Merchant Taylors' School, then in the old building over the road. The building survived as a farmhouse until it was demolished in 1936, and its place has been taken by a funeral director.

Liverpool Road Methodist Church
Constructed in 1863, due to the growth of the congregation the church was rebuilt in 1890 on Mersey Road using recycled materials. This can be observed most emphatically in the main doorways, which have been reused in the church hall facing on to Brompton Avenue, although one pillar (inset) has had to be replicated. Two crenulated gateposts remain by the church hall, but others have been lost along with the rest of the wall in the construction of the bypass.

Methodist Church Hall

Some of the congregation were unhappy at the move to Mersey Road from Liverpool Road and continued to worship in the church hall, the corner of which appears on the right of the photograph above. From 1988 it served as the Crossroads Centre, run by the Crosby Group of Churches, and transferred in 1993 to a new building on the St Luke's site. It is now used for commercial purposes. Buildings beyond the hall have made way for the bypass, as can be seen in the more recent photograph with the corner of the building visible to the right.

CROSBY VILLAGE, CROSBY

C. 6514

Coronation Road School
We look down Coronation Road towards the park. On the right stands Crosby County Secondary School for Boys, which closed when it merged with Waterloo Park Grammar School to form Chesterfield High School in 1972. The building was then occupied by Vale School until its amalgamation with Sherwood School to become Valewood. On the right is Banner's stonemasons yard, compulsorily purchased to make way for the new bypass, with the school site now occupied by retirement home, Sandalwood.

Central Buildings

We look up Coronation Road towards Central Buildings on the left, victim of the property speculation that led up to the financial crisis of 2008, and on the right Crown Buildings, resilient survivor of the ravages of developers. On the immediate left is Coronation Road School, and on the right, beyond the shops, Livock and Edwards' garage, now demolished and replaced by a Tesco Express. Note the railings to prevent the pupils from spilling out onto the road.

Coronation Park Entrance

Above is a view before the boulder stone was moved here in 1926 by traction engine. The Blundell family gave land to the people of Crosby as a 'recreation ground' alongside Thorps Lane, as it was known then. The name was changed to Coronation Road to celebrate the coronation of Edward VII and Queen Alexandra, and the Recreation Ground received its present name in 1906. The original ornate ironwork may have been sacrificed to the First World War effort.

RECREATION GROUND, Gt CROSBY. C.49.

Coronation Park

Lack of adult supervision and the formality of the school uniforms indicate a bygone age, but not before 1906, as the title suggests. Brass bands used to play in the park bandstand, and a bowling green and tennis courts enhance the facilities until this day. The basic playground equipment has changed little in decades but fashions have, as in the scene of the boating lake opened in 1931. Remote-controlled boats now compete for space with sail.

Coronation Road Shops

Opposite the entrance to Coronation Park, the attractive arcades have disappeared and the entire shops, bar one, have changed in character. Satterthwaite's family-run bakery and headquarters from 1920 were on the extreme left of this row of shops. For nearly a century, their cakes and pies were a special treat in their seven shops in Crosby, but recently it became a casualty in the closure of local, long-standing businesses. However, such was the strength of the brand that it has reopened under the same name but with new management.

York Avenue

Off the main streets, a typical suburban scene of the early part of the last century is recorded. The aproned boy could be delivering from Satterthwaite's, just off the picture in the old photograph, but visible to the right in the recent scene. Child chair, hat, long skirt and handcart have given way to pushchair, bare head, trousers and white van. The trees have grown, if they have not been uprooted, but the decorative porch and a gatepost survive in the house on the immediate right.

St Luke's Church

A photograph from the 1860s or 1870s has the earliest known representation of the 1859 vicarage (back left), replaced in 1971. St Luke's church was consecrated on Boxing Day 1853 to replace St Michael's chapel, which was becoming too small for the growing population. Although badly damaged by fire in 1972, the spire remains intact, as seen in the photograph to the right. Below, a cannon, a relic left over from the time when merchant ships had to arm themselves against piracy in the early 1800s, protects the corner of the graveyard wall. In the nineteenth century, the wall was subjected to damage by the wheels of carts using the weighbridge at the front of the Crosby Hotel.

St Luke's Vicarage

Revd Robert Love, vicar of St Luke's 1870–1902, presides over tennis on the vicarage lawn wearing a top hat. At the back can be seen the transept of the church, which survived the fire of 1972 with its walls intact, but had to be reroofed and was indeed reroofed again in 2010 prior to internal reordering. Now, the garden is used by many different people and here they are making giant puppets for an outdoor dramatic event, with the church still glimpsed through the trees.

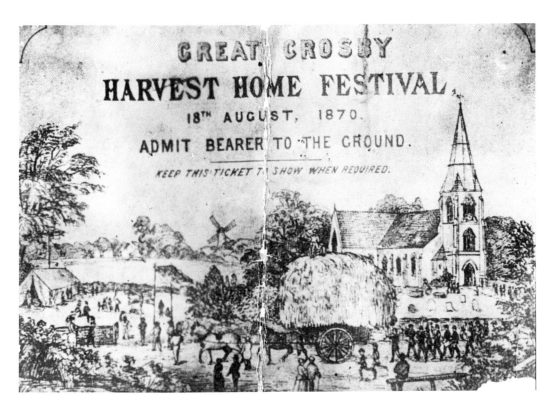

GREAT CROSBY
HARVEST HOME FESTIVAL,
18TH AUGUST, 1870.
ADMIT BEARER TO THE GROUND.

KEEP THIS TICKET TO SHOW WHEN REQUIRED.

St Luke's Graveyard

The ticket illustrates the still rural scene of Crosby in 1870, with St Luke's church and the mill in Moor Lane clearly shown. Allowing for some artistic licence, the festival appears to occupy land later used for the expanding graveyard, which accommodates 6,000 plots with about 20,000 burials, now restricted to members of the church. Interesting graves include twin sisters with a combined age of 200 and a memorial to 'Bertie', who died on the *Titanic*. The church and graveyard are instantly recognisable from the same viewpoint today.

PARISH OF
ST LUKE
GREAT CROSBY

St Luke's Interior

St Luke's Victorian Gothic chancel was destroyed by fire in 1972. Fortunately, the glorious transept windows dating from 1866 to 1884, designed by Capronnier and made in Brussels, were saved and restored. The Good Samaritan window and the reordering of the church in 2011 feature in the photograph below. The window commemorates John Myers, a wealthy landowner and one of the main benefactors of the church, who laid the foundation stone of the church in 1853.

Merchant Taylors' School for Girls Library

The only Grade II* listed building in Crosby and the oldest by far in the township, dating from 1620, is pictured in the late nineteenth century in its then countrified setting. John Harrison senior, born in Crosby in 1530, became a successful wool merchant and entered the Merchant Taylors' Company (a Guild) in London. His son John followed him into the successful business, and when he died childless in 1619, left money to found Merchant Taylors' School (for boys) as a supreme act of gratitude and faith. When the new boys' school was constructed in the 1880s, the building was handed over to the girls' school, founded in 1888. It is now their library. Over the entrance was the 'birch room' where the boys were punished. Though unchanged externally, it is now surrounded by much newer buildings.

The Mulberries

Behind and to the right of the 1920s hockey team can be seen the mulberry, probably planted when the eponymous residence was built in the 1840s. In 1911, this large adjacent house and garden was acquired by Merchant Taylors' School for Girls, and adapted to extend the school and increase sports provision. Since the original tree fell down, its place has been taken by another, to the right of the recent photograph, affording shelter to succeeding generations.

Liverpool Road Widening

The safety and constructional methods (courtesy of the *Crosby Herald*) of this operation make interesting viewing. When Liverpool Road was widened in 1929, part of Merchant Taylors' School for Girls was demolished and the building realigned. The imposing doorway that had been added at the same time as the acquisition of The Mulberries in 1911 was retained, and can be seen incorporated into the new vitreum of 2009, beyond which can be seen the block realigned in 1929.

The Regent Cinema

Advertising Ethel Clayton in *Young Mrs Winthrop* soon after it opened in 1920, the Regent Cinema was the largest in the area, accommodating 825 in the stalls and 250 in the balcony. Notice the upstairs café. Closed in 1968 and converted into a bingo hall, it is now St Mary's College Sports Centre. Next door is the original parish hall of St Luke's, used as the Picture House from 1913–16, now the Comrades Club following the building of the new parish hall in 1970.

ENDBUTT LANE, G.T. CROSBY   2240

The Endbutt Hotel and Bethel Church

The hotel of 1924 and the church of 1914 are unchanged in appearance to this day. Endbutt Lane leads to the Leeds & Liverpool Canal, at one time the best way into Liverpool. The origin of the Endbutt Hotel is, surprisingly, associated with Methodism. In 1910, Methodists met in a building that had been designed as a public house, but refused a licence. When they left it for their purpose-built chapel (now the Bethel Independent Methodist church) in Seafield Avenue, the original, neglected, pub building was demolished and the present premises opened in 1924.

St Mary's College

The eagle of the American coat of arms (inset) emblazoned on the gateposts proclaims connections with the United States. Claremont House was built by a Liverpool merchant, who was also a representative and double agent of the Southern States during the American Civil War. A Confederate spy, James D. Bulloch, lived here and it was the home of the United States consul in Liverpool. In 1919, the Christian Brothers established the Catholic Institute in the house, which then became their nursery school after new buildings were added to form St Mary's College in 1924.

Convent S.H.M. Seafield, Gt Crosby, Liverpool
A Class Room.

Seafield

Classroom interiors and uniforms have changed since these photographs were taken, but the exterior of the front of the building remains as impressively solid as ever. The Religious Order of the Sacred Heart of Mary founded a school in Bootle in 1872, moving into Seafield House, which had been built as a hotel in Seaforth in 1884. In 1908, it moved into its new buildings in Crosby to be known as Seafield Catholic Grammar School for Girls. In 1977 it was amalgamated with St Bede's Secondary School (in Myers Road East) to form Sacred Heart Comprehensive School, named after the order of its original foundation.

Convent S.H.M. Seafield, Gt Crosby, Liverpool
South Wing

Stanfield Preparatory School, Crosby, Lancs.

Stanfield

The original character of a private residence has been preserved through two educational manifestations. Marked Standfield on the Ordnance Survey map of 1907, it was home of the Thorougood family, brewers, and then adapted as a school. In 1945 it was taken over by Merchant Taylors' School for Girls as their junior department. Since then a technology block has been added (below), which sits rather incongruously beside it, and further changes are planned.

St Peter and St Paul's

The old church, built in 1826, was replaced further back from the road by the present one in 1894. Its beautiful interior has stone Corinthian columns, Gothic arches and a magnificent pulpit by Augustus Pugin, originally in St Mary's, Lumber Street, Liverpool. The adjacent burial ground has some striking monuments. Here are interred the chief benefactors of the church, Peter McKinley and his wife Catherine, together with her sister, the mother of Father James Nugent, outstanding philanthropist and benefactor of the poor in Liverpool.

Merchant Taylors' School

On sports day in about 1905, a large crowd of parents and visitors in their finery stand around with bunting flying freely. Smartly dressed staff supervise, and a band provides extra entertainment and spectacle. Several items of kit appear to have been abandoned on the ground – just like current sports days! St Faith's church is in the background, and the original pavilion of 1895 is in front of it. The 1912 replacement of this (left below) still stands today. In spite of being dwarfed by a new sports centre, the charming old cricket pavilion has, with commendable respect for tradition and preservation of heritage buildings, been blended into the total design. The school was founded in 1620 in the building now used by Merchant Taylors' School for Girls as a library. Their new building was opened on the present site in 1878.

Rossett Road

This cul-de-sac, an early offshoot from College Road, is still quiet ('quite' in the message written on the card), except on alternate Saturdays as it runs alongside the ground of what used to be one of the leading amateur football clubs, Marine. They moved to Rossett Park (now the Arriva Stadium) in 1903 and reached the Amateur Cup Final in 1932. In 1992, they reached the third round of the FA Cup for the first time. Their record attendance of 4,000 was against Nigeria in 1949. Rossett Road, unchanged, runs by the side of the football ground from bottom left to right in the aerial view (courtesy of the *Crosby Herald*). The boxer Nel Tarleton lived at No. 15 (white fronted, seventh right-handed semi-detached house along).

Carnegie Library

An imposing domed clock tower proclaims importance and demands attention; a handsome entrance through Classical columns surmounted by a renaissance dome welcomes the reader; a light, lofty interior with Classical decoration sets the tone for learning; the Dutch gable on the left of the asymmetrical façade reflects Alexandra Hall (visible to the left) which composes, with the Congregational church opposite, a trio of majestic buildings. Yet the library, opened in 1905 with a grant from Andrew Carnegie, steel magnate and philanthropist, faces closure.

LAYING OF THE FOUNDATION STONE OF THE
PRESENT CHURCH, 22nd MAY, 1897.

Congregational Church

It is a top-hatted occasion, even for the gentleman on a horse, as A. Brown Paton, a member
of the church, lays the foundation stone. Interspersed are boaters and bowlers, while hats for
the ladies are *de rigueur*. Now the church, United Reformed since 1972, hides the houses at the
start of Eshe Road but the mature trees of Alexandra Park can be glimpsed to the right of the
recent photograph.

Alexandra Hall and Park

The young trees of the park have not yet screened the rear Dutch gable of the hall and the Gothic gable of the Congregational church. Crosby became an Urban District Council in 1894, adopted the Assembly Rooms (opened in 1888) as its headquarters, and in 1902 renamed them Alexandra Hall. The Beatles performed here in 1961 before they topped the charts. The apartment block replacing the hall in 2004 cleverly echoes the demarcation, dimensions, design, decoration and denotation (Alexandra Court) of the original.

Carnival Procession and May Queen

Judged by the fashions and the period telephone box, the photographs date from the 1920s. Above, Britannia, patriotically and appropriately advertising Robert Walmsley (removal and cartage contractor), pauses outside Alexandra Hall, the Town Hall of Crosby in its glory days. An enthusiastic crowd of all ages and an official look on. Below, the May Queen is sponsored by George Stanton, Motors and Wedding Carriage (Marsh Lane, Bootle) and Private Motor Ambulance. Travelling in style, she is admired by ladies dressed suitably for the occasion.

Fire Brigade

The knot of bystanders indicates that the fire brigade, in ceremonial attire, is taking part in a carnival. It is passing the triangle of ground at the back of the Carnegie Library. The open space to the left is now occupied by a utility building; a capping stone – at least – of the gateposts to the path survives. The brigade will return to their headquarters on the other side of Alexandra Park, now redeveloped as Fire Station Close (inset).

Wright's Pit, Crosby.

The Duck Pond

Pram-walker and horses look
at each other across the pond
through decorative railings.
This is a remnant of one of
the many pits in Crosby dug
out to extract marl clay to
fertilise the fields. It became
part of Wright's Big Pit Farm,
which survived as a dairy
when the farmland was sold
off for housing – until the
buildings were demolished
to make way for Mere Park
flats in the 1960s. The elegant
railings survive intact.

War Damage

This is the scene that met an ARP warden when he arrived home after duty. His house, No. 22 Bonnington Avenue, had been hit by a high explosive bomb; his wife and two children (one destined to go to Oxford University) had been killed, the first deaths in Crosby in the Second World War. Crosby was not a target for bombing (except possibly for Littlewoods), but suffered collateral damage from raids on nearby Bootle and Liverpool docks. The house has been perfectly rebuilt.

Bus Station

Passengers wait patiently for the driver to admit them to an extended 30 service from Netherton to Walton Hospital on its first day of operation in 1962. Worked by the Merseyside Passenger Transport Executive, it was the first time an operator other than Ribble had used their bus station. The station, with minimal facilities, opened in 1938, was rebuilt in the 1970s, and closed by 1990 when the new terminus was opened in Islington. Aintree University Hospital is now the main provider for hospital care for Crosbeians, who still, however, tend to refer to it by its old name Fazakerley; this is the title advertised on the 122 Avon service direction indicator as it passes the site now occupied by a tyre firm.

Moor Lane by the Mill

In the year this was taken, you could sit on a bench with not a car in sight and enjoy a country view with wooden palisade railings and young roadside trees. There is evidence of horse-drawn traffic and you could take a path (now Poplar Avenue) through a gate into fields. A later view shows the effect of the increase of motor traffic along the main road from Liverpool to Southport. Trees have grown and others been replaced; Poplar Avenue has been developed, and telephone and post boxes built.

THE OLD MILL AND MOOR LANE, CROSBY.   H.9947.

Crosby Mill

When it was completed in 1814, the mill quickly became a landmark for sailors. Steam and then gas were used as auxiliary power until 1910, when severe gales destroyed the gearing. The sails were removed in 1922, but the mill continued working until 1972. Plans for demolition and development as a housing estate were staved off when a local builder, Tony Lock, adapted it for living accommodation. Now, a continual stream of traffic makes it difficult to cross the road.

The Nag's Head

The clothing of the figures defines their status in this idyllic rural scene set in the 1890s. By the early years of the last century, both the thatched and brick buildings had been replaced by the present central part of the building, with an attractive covering of creeper forming the backdrop to the scene below. The service run by the Lancashire & Yorkshire Railway from its station to Thornton was only short lived. What is the relationship of the 'driver' to the two family groups, which includes a grandfather and twin grandsons?

Thornton Stocks and Sundial

Once, the main road was just a country lane, with only a hedge and wooden railings to protect the stocks and sundial. Damaged by a car during the blackout in the Second World War, they were stored away, then repaired and safeguarded on their original site by an iron palisade. Sympathetic additions have also been made to the Nag's Head. Replaced in 1791, the stocks were used as early as 1725 and as late as 1863. The sundial possibly dates from the early eighteenth century.

Sefton Church

The fourteenth-century spire and sixteenth-century nave are outstandingly beautiful, and the church has been called 'Cathedral of the Fields' or 'the Jewel of South West Lancashire' – although criticism has been expressed of the heavy pinnacles attached to the tower. Dating from 1170, St Helen's church in Sefton village is the mother and grandmother church of twenty-nine others in the area. The village, in a central and neutral position in the area and of great historic interest, was chosen in 1974 to give its name to the Metropolitan Borough of Sefton, in which the church is the only Grade I listed building. The early nineteenth-century print engraved by W. Taylor shows a lady looking at a tombstone with the inscription 'John Harwood [the artist] born 12 July 1798', while a mysterious procession heads towards the church. The church remains unchanged (photography by O. Yandell, Rector 1973–91).

Sefton Church Interior

The woodcarving of the end of the pews, the pulpit and the screen is especially fine, and the monuments of the Molyneux family from Sefton and Croxteth who patronised the church comprise the best series in Lancashire. Others buried here are the Blundells of Crosby and Ince Blundell, and John Sadler, who discovered the secrets of transfer printing on pottery. Open days organised by the Friends of Sefton raise funds with quizzes encouraging visitors to look at the wealth of artistic and historical interest.

Ince Blundell Hall

Careful composition of the shooting party draws attention to the 'Pantheon', appropriately added to the hall (on the right) to house a collection of Roman statues. Collected by Henry Blundell from the 1760s onwards, they were also exhibited in a 'temple' in Classical style built in the garden (inset) and are now on display in the Walker Art Gallery in Liverpool. The hall was built by the Weld Blundells between 1720 and 1750. After military occupation during the war, it was bought by the Augustinian Sisters in 1960, who converted it into a nursing home.

Blundellsands and Crosby Station

This is the grander side of the station looking towards the Blundellsands estate, with a porte cochère covering the carriages waiting for the trains from Liverpool. The above image was taken during the changeover period between horse and petrol power, probably in the 1920s. The first section of the Liverpool, Crosby and Southport Railway was opened between Waterloo and Southport in 1848. The station building has now been replaced, and the coal yard converted into a car park.

Blundellsands and Crosby Station

The attire of waiting passengers, advice to third class passengers wishing to smoke, gas lighting, magnificent canopies and two uniformed station staff waiting for the train comprise a typical Edwardian railway scene. The station (on the first main line to be electrified in Britain) was some distance from Crosby, as the landowning Blundells offered land free to the railway on the unproductive sand dune area nearer the sea to keep it away from the village and Crosby Hall.

Blundellsands Hotel

With its impressive baronial hall façade, for well over a century the hotel was the social centre of Blundellsands, affording the only public bar in the area and reception rooms for weddings and other celebrations. Liverpool and Everton football clubs held dinners here, and the variety of notable guests is said to have included the Duke of Edinburgh, Sir Richard Attenborough and Wilfred Owen. Lack of demand for its hotel facilities led to its closure in 1999 and conversion in 2001 into apartments with extensions.

Lansdowne

It is interesting to speculate on the relationships and status of the figures in the archive photograph. Lansdowne House started life as a grand residential house in prime position by the station. It was then adapted as a maternity nursing home and in 1978 converted into a halfway house. Now in a state of decay, it is a target for vandalism, on sale with planning permission for thirteen apartments.

Mersey Road Methodist Church

The horse-drawn cart and painter oblivious of safety practice date this photograph. Beyond is the Dutch gable of Alexandra Hall. Bricks from the rugged Romanesque tower of the Methodist church in Liverpool Road have been recycled into a graceful Gothic spire, and two resurrected doorways are set into the hall in Brompton Avenue (inset). Bomb damage in 1941 led to the demolition of the spire, and the church was remodelled after an outbreak of fire on the very eve of its centenary celebration in 1991.

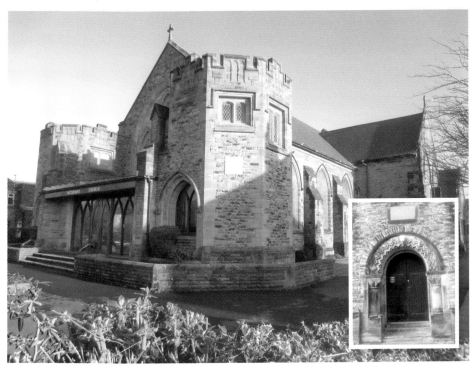

St Barnabas' and St Nicholas' Churches

This iron church dedicated to St Barnabas was erected in 1864 on the tongue of land along Mersey Road between the ends of Warren Road and Agnes Road. In 1874, it was replaced by St Nicholas' church opposite. On the left, in the distance off Agnes Road are Rabbit Road (Weld Road since 1927) and Anchorage, which still stands on the north side. Beyond is the row of houses in Blundellsands Road East, now extending from Eshe Road North to College Road North, with Wright's Farm (now the Duck Pond) among the trees. In the detail of the photograph below, to the right of the church is the stationmaster's house, situated at the level crossing by the first station before the Mersey Road bridge was built. Between the church and house can be seen St Michael's Tower, since removed, which then stood midway along Islington. On the extreme right is the spire of St Luke's church, almost hiding the windmill, with its original working sails. To the left of this can be seen the tower of Liverpool Road Methodist church.

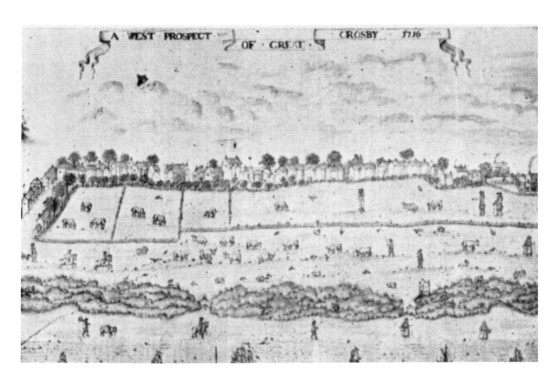

St Nicholas' Church

Ships are sailing, and people walking or riding along the beach, into Liverpool; rabbits frolic in the sandhills and beyond the fields is Crosby village; on the right is the 1620 Merchant Taylors' School building and the taller building left of centre may be the St Michael's chapel, which preceded the one built in 1770. This plaque, destroyed in the Second World War, survives through photographs. Below are St Nicholas' church and the Mersey Road incline to the railway bridge, the steepest in the area!

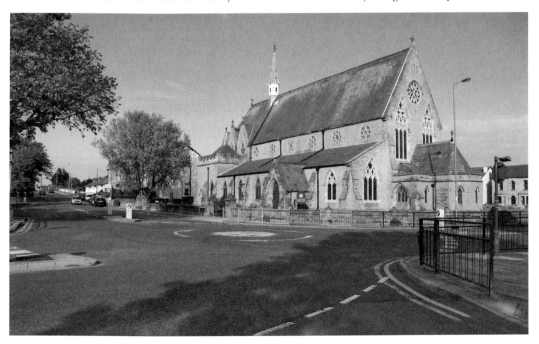

Crosby Station

An all-male cast (except for one of Dr May's daughters) faces the camera at Crosby station, as it was first called, in the early 1880s. The signalman has turned the wheel to close the gates at the level crossing, but the signal is still in the stop position. Taken after the station was moved to Blundellsands Road from Mersey Road, the engine has run around its train and is returning to Liverpool. Modern stock passes the old stationmaster's house as it approaches Mersey Road bridge.

Pattison and Davies

Mr C. C. Pattison senior is standing in the doorway of his shop, Nos. 31–33 Bridge Road, on some special occasion, maybe the Silver Jubilee of 1935 or the Coronation of 1937. Established in 1889, it is now a discount food and wine store, much altered in appearance and appeal. Below is an advertisement which appeared in the Grand Bazaar programme of St Luke's church on 1–3 November 1928 for him and R. C. ('Ricky') Davies, whose premises were a few doors away.

80

Established 1889. Telephone 291 Crosby.	Telephone 432 Crosby. ESTIMATES GIVEN.
C. C. PATTISON,	**R. C. DAVIES,**
HIGH CLASS	Upholsterer and
WINE & SPIRIT MERCHANT.	General House Furnisher.
FAMILY ALES AND STOUT. WHISKIES, BRANDIES, WINES AND MINERALS. CIGARS AND TOBACCO, &c.	Settees. Curtains. Decorations for Dances Easy Chairs. Blinds. Receptions, &c., Re-Upholstering. Repairs. a speciality.
31 and 33 BRIDGE ROAD, BLUNDELLSANDS.	**41 BRIDGE ROAD, BLUNDELLSANDS.**

Bridge Road Shops

Traffic then was almost exclusively horse-drawn, handcarts and cycles. Now the Blundellsands post office and Lewis Bros, butchers, on either side of Cavendish Road, and Hepburns garage on the left are no more. But the fine dormer windows here and up the road survive, and a biker is heading for Ben Lloyd's cycle shop. This, together with wine and spirit merchant C. C. Pattison, next to it, and further along chemist Hamers, composes an impressive trio of shops still in the same line of business for over a century. In the distance is the tower of Treleavan.

Treleavan

Students from Sandford can safely pose by the lamp post at the intersection of Dowhills Road and Blundellsands Road West. Apart from the lamp post, long since removed, the view remains remarkably recognisable. An imposing gateway leads to the huge turreted Treleavan. Now converted into apartments, it was designed for Nicholas Blundell by T. Mellard Reade, who laid out the Blundellsands estate in 1868. As well as an architect and civil engineer, Reade was also a noted geologist who debated the age of the Earth.

Blundellsands Road West

Where the road meets the sea, straight from the station, smartly dressed girls are going down to the shore and fashionable ladies are silhouetted on the sandhills. A boat in full sail bespeaks the era. Right and left behind high walls and trees lie secluded Victorian mansions: Weston (left), and The Downs and Ramleh (right), home of Sir William Forwood with its fountains and, like the others, magnificent views over the Mersey. All now have been replaced by apartment blocks of the same name, but remnants of their solid walls survive. Below, Weston Court is to the left, overlooking water outfall works in progress with relics of its old wall in the foreground and New Brighton over the Mersey in the distance.

Presbyterian Church

Fashions and relationships between churches in Liverpool have changed much since this wedding group of 1930 posed outside the Presbyterian (now United Reformed) church in Warren Road. Behind and over the road is St Joseph's Roman Catholic church, opened in 1886, and its presbytery of 1890. It is pictured below with the Presbyterian church on the right. Before the present Gothic stone building was constructed in 1905, the Presbyterians had met in Alexandra Hall and an iron church in Serpentine South.

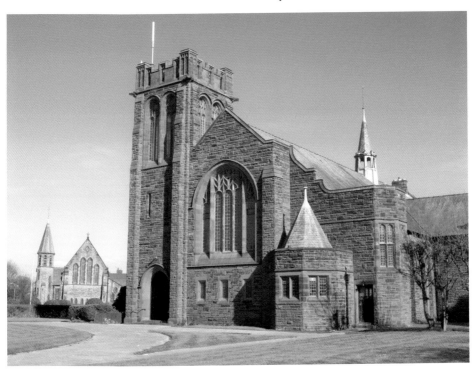

St Nicholas Fountain

Above the postbox beautifully designed into the wall, a notice advertises that a grand Victorian mansion, The Glen, is for sale. Like so many others, it has now been replaced by an apartment block, Fountains Court. Joseph Gardner, a wealthy timber merchant who lived nearby, is said to have been plagued by 'Cockle Mollies' and fishermen from the beach asking for water. In 1881 he built the fountain, inscribed appropriately with words from St John's Gospel 4.13–14 'Whosoever drinketh...'

St. Nicholas Fountain, Blundell Sands.

Burbo Bank Road North

We are looking north along Burbo Bank Road North, named after one of the sandbanks alongside the shipping channel in the Mersey estuary at this point. The Glen is on the right, and beyond peer the pinnacles of Uplands. Above the trees to the left may be seen the top of a house bordering the shore. This was to be washed into the sea along with others, owing to erosion caused by the outflow of the River Alt. Today, a stretch of green extends to the coastguard station with its communications mast, now closed.

Beachside Towers

The house has lost most of its garden, and Netherwood next door is beginning to crumble. In the early years of the twentieth century, grandiose houses lined the shore along the west side of Burbo Bank Road North. By 1921 the sea had begun to take its toll, and by 1927 only the ominously named Edgewater was still standing. Similar houses on the other side of the Serpentine – Emrow and Cap Martin – have survived.

Seafront

A makeshift car park has been formed from rubble left over from houses eroded by the sea. Traces can still be seen of its entrance from the Serpentine. The style of car indicates the date (late 1950s), before the sea-wall defences were constructed. In the distance is The Glen, now superseded by the thirty apartments of Fountains Court. A panoramic photograph taken from the same place today shows, from left to right: the head of an iron man peeping out from the sea; a container ship leaving the Mersey channel; waves dashing against the promenade; the mile marker standing between sea and sky; the coastguard station with its communications mast; the tall white block of Burbo Point; the low profile modern development along Burbo Bank Road North; and finally two apartment blocks replacing Victorian properties, Fountains Court in white and Holyrood in red.

Blundellsands Beach

Young Edwardian ladies and gentlemen in their beachwear! In the background are silhouetted some of the Victorian residences that graced the seashore, soon to be destroyed by advancing erosion. In contrast, looking the other way from the same spot, a girl plays with Antony Gormley's replica, one of the iron men forming a pattern on the beach. The backcloth of modernity has all been created since the Edwardian photograph with one possible exception (the Liver Building). From left to right: the cranes of the Seaforth container dock (merging into the Anglican Cathedral 5 miles away), the beacon of St John's market in the city centre, the Liver Building (constructed in 1907), the wind turbines and the radar tower.

Shipwreck

The Russian barque *Matador* from Riga foundered in October 1902 following a severe gale. The crew of nine had been rescued by the Hilbre lifeboat based on the Wirral at the mouth of the River Dee; the coxswain was awarded a silver medal, and the crew a First Class Certificate for Life Saving on Waters. In the distance can be seen the tower at New Brighton which, when completed in 1900, was the highest building in Britain at 567 feet (173 meters). In one of the many varied views that can be enjoyed from the seafront, sunset silhouettes the buildings of New Brighton across the Mersey on a calm winter evening but (inset) a storm batters the sea defences.

BLUNDELLSAND SHORE   1436.

Speed Markers

Almost miraculously, one of the markers for speed tests erected in 1865 by Mariners Road and Hall Road has survived sea and weather. Measuring one mile between them with a pair at each point so that exact sightings could be made, all but one were removed when the sea wall was built in the 1970s. Cargo ships, such as the one between the markers, have been superseded by fewer, larger vessels and ever more tonnage passes through Liverpool docks.

Patterns on the Shore

In the distance, the base of the New Brighton Tower is silhouetted against the sky. It was dismantled by 1921, although its ballroom continued in use until destroyed by fire in 1969. The speed markers opposite Mariners Road stand sentinel over the tents looking like a military encampment. Patterning of a different kind celebrated the passing of the Olympic torch through the Borough of Sefton when 5,963 pupils from more than fifty-one schools took part in a successful attempt to form the largest human Olympic ring (courtesy of Andrew Teebay, *Crosby Herald*).

Jack Johnson

The Hermit of the Sandhills or Cockler Johnson, a veteran of the Crimean War, built a hut on the foreshore as home for himself and his wife. It was built of wood with a brick chimney and rainwater was collected from the roof. He lived here for over thirty years as a local celebrity. The coastguard station nearby has recently been closed and the military appearance of the old coastguards is a reminder of how their role has changed.

West Lancashire Golf Club

The club, founded in 1873, is the ninth oldest in the country. Members pose in 1888 outside the original clubhouse, which was situated where Dowhills Park apartments are now by Hall Road station (below). The barriers, now remotely controlled from a signal centre by Sandhills station, have replaced the cumbersome, but enthralling, gates operated manually from the signal box alongside. In the 1920s, Blundellsands could boast, in addition to golf, two tennis clubs, the rugby club and an archery association.

West Lancashire Golf Clubhouses
A steam train passes the 1893 clubhouse, designed by T. Mellard Reade, which replaced the original beside the railway line at Hall Road. The nine-hole course extended from there alongside the east of the railway line towards Hightown. In 1922, nine holes were added on the other side of the line which was crossed by a footbridge. From 1891, the ladies had their own course on the west of the line and from 1947 their clubhouse was the still-surviving Brooklyn, Hall Road West. In 1961, the courses on the west side of the line were combined with a new clubhouse and the original men's course on the east side was sold for housing.

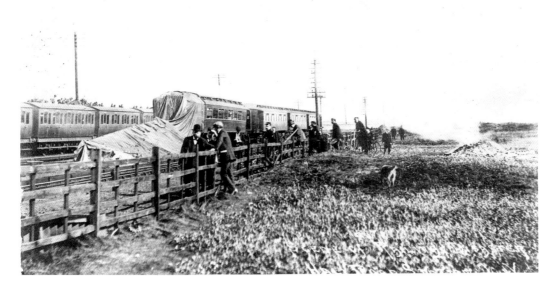

Hall Road Station

The crash of 1907 that killed twenty people was caused by a signalman's error, when an express ploughed into a local train terminating at the station. This is on the very edge of the Liverpool conurbation. Initially, the railway company had refused Joseph Gardner's request to build a station for his house alone, so he built five more to reach the quota. To the left of the view below is the new golf clubhouse and the remains of the old workshops, now demolished.

Waterloo Rugby Football Club

A carnival of yesteryear contrasts with a recent match. The club was founded in 1882, and known as Serpentine after the road near its original ground. In 1884, a dispute prompted relocation to Waterloo; the club's name was changed accordingly and stayed when the club returned to Blundellsands in 1892. In its heyday, the ground entertained international touring sides, and in 1977 the club reached the final of the John Player knockout competition. However, the club failed to attract sufficient sponsorship when professionalism came in, and has dropped down from premier level to a steady position in National League 3 North.

St Michael's Church

Graced, appropriately, with a lychgate, St Michael's was planted in open country in 1907 as a mission church of St Luke's, anticipating the housing development that was going to take place. The iron church ('tin tabernacle') had previously been used as the hall for nearby St Nicholas'. Relegated to hall status again when the brick church was built in 1931, it was finally replaced by a companion brick hall in 1961. The lychgate retired to a new country home.

NICHOLAS BLUNDELL ESQ^{RE}
PLAN OF PROPOSED CONVERSION OF SCHOOL
AT CROSBY INTO A HOUSE .

FRONT ELEVATION

Boundary Cottage
The building was originally a school
built by William Blundell for the Roman
Catholic children of Little Crosby. From
1859 until 1887, when a new school
was built for them, it was occupied
by Yeomanry under the command of
Squire, later Colonel, Nicholas Blundell.
The present house takes its name from
the much-disputed boundary brook that
used to separate the two Crosbies. It is
now piped under the road, but marked
by the Boundary Stone, defaced during
the war to mislead invaders.

Little Crosby Church

A procession lines up to go into the church, supervised by the nuns who used to live at the convent. St Mary's church, consecrated in 1847, was built in early Decorated style with stone obtained nearby from the delph (quarry) by Delph Lane. It superseded the chapel in West Lane House (left of the church), which was then altered to be used as a presbytery, convent and school until 1963, when the new school was built just over the road.

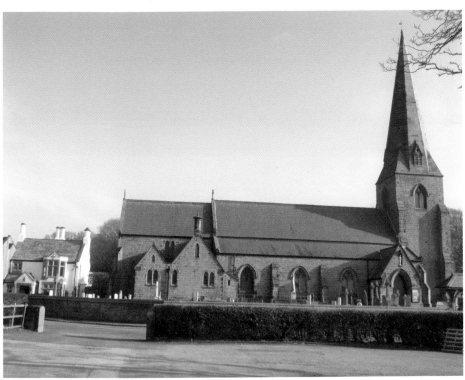

Little Crosby Cross

The pump, installed to draw water from the village well in 1616, is visible, though disused, on the photograph of 1892. A cross has been here for over 300 years, and at some point one was set over the well, as still seen today. For centuries, this area was part of the village green, but in 1857 it was enclosed by a wall to make gardens for the adjacent cottages and the well cross moved to its present position.

Little Crosby Village

Time to gossip over the front garden wall or just stand and stare; freedom to walk arm in arm or set up one's easel in the road; the only traffic a small cart: Squire Colonel Nicholas Blundell painted this watercolour of the leisurely, peaceful life of Little Crosby in the 1860s. Now speed bumps try to slow commuters avoiding the busy main road between Crosby and Southport, but the buildings of Little Crosby have changed little in a century and a half.

Crosby Hall

William Blundell (Squire, 1894–1909) sits in a relaxed mood holding a dog in a very early chain driven car, while earlier still in the 1860s (inset) the younger members of the family are taken for a ride accompanied by their Nanny. In contrast the present Squire Mark Blundell stands by one of the family cars at the front of the hall. The ornate Victorian porch has now been removed to revert to the appearance of the original 1609 building.

Crosby Hall

We are looking at the back of the hall, home of the Blundells of Crosby for over 400 years, in about 1900. In this scene, the dog sits in prime position guarding the figures standing by the garden entrance to the original building of about 1609. Since this date, Victorian wings have been added (to right and left of picture). In 1953–55, alterations and demolition restored it to its former dignified and symmetrical structure, as seen below. The gardens host several events during the year, the most notable being an outdoor production of a classic play when the audience can enjoy interval refreshments on the lawn.

Crosby Hall Educational Trust

Visitors are being shown round the Home Farm at Crosby Hall by Francis Nicholas Blundell (Squire, 1909–36), on the right of the photograph. The barn has now been adapted for social occasions, and the adjacent outbuildings converted for the use of Crosby Hall Educational Centre (CHET). These now afford residential facilities, particularly for school groups to enjoy and appreciate the countryside though outdoor activities. Here, open day visitors enjoy refreshments in the courtyard.

Little Crosby Agriculture

Even the horses pose statuesquely and seriously in celebration of a bumper harvest ready for the road. In such a barn Bob Wright, from a local farming family, created a museum in Little Crosby to house agricultural equipment and relics of bygone days. Pictured here with some of his exhibits, he devoted his life to preserving the heritage of Crosby, but sadly, both he and his collection have now passed away (courtesy of David Brownless, www.davebrownlee.com).

River Alt

Dinghies belonging to the Blundellsands Sailing Club are moored on the River Alt around 1925, on the bend of the river to the right of the modern aerial photograph (courtesy of the *Crosby Herald*). This shows how sand dunes in the area have since been covered by housing. The River Alt winds its way to the sea and is still forming a channel along the shore, but erosion at Blundellsands has been stopped by a barrier diverting its waters to the sea.